Aspire Poems

ASPIRE POEMS

Arnold David Richards

International Psychoanalytic Books
New York • http://www.IPBooks.net

Aspire, Poems by Arnold David Richards

Published by IPBooks, Queens, NY
Online at IPBooks.net

Cover Painting: El Lissitzky, *About Two Squares* (1922).
Cover Design: Blackthorn Studio
Typesetting: Noel S. Morao

ISBN: 978-1-956864-99-1

Renaissance Man

When you meet a man of all seasons
With a broad knowledge base
Who has expertise in many fields
Incisive intellectual curiosity
Who is creative in both science and art

You have met a "man for all seasons"
A man true to his principles and conscience
A fighter for social justice
Who refuses to cave to public pressure
Who teaches what he preaches

When you meet Dr. Arnold Richards
In person, in his books and writing
And in this poetry
You have met an intellect with heart
You have met a Renaissance man.

—JUDITH LOGUE, PHD, psychoanalyst, Founding Member, IPPNJ
(Institute for Psychoanalysis & Psychotherapy of New Jersey)

Contents

Free Association

they are determined by a lifetime of other thoughts
and a lifetime of experience
in fact it is those determinants
they provide us with access
to our unconscious
what we hide from others
and what we hide from ourselves
there is a lot we can't remember
a lot we would rather not remember
but what we can't remember
we can't forget
our minds have three layers
conscious pre conscious and unconscious
conscious is accessible
precocious is our Siri
or our google
my interest is in where is our creative part
some of it is located where we sleep
our dreams
part is in our hypnopompic
state of mind
between sleeping and waking
we access a large world
it is the world that allows the poet to write poetry
the musician to write music
it should be cherished and nurtured
it will sustain us for our whole life

Justice

is often hard to come by
those in charge
pursue their own interests
governments especially
steal from the poor
and give to the rich
Communism was supposed to be the solution
but it wasn't
millions murdered
a god that failed
laws can help
impartial courts can help
our only resort
and cooperation
and demonstration
and the power of the pen
power to the people

Arnold David Richards

Pluralism

is profound
the basis of democracy
of our country
the declaration of independence
all are created equal
wars fought
Civil War
World War II
deny the existence of a group
if one group is denied
all are at risk
i thought our country had its act together
after the second world war
but pluralism is being undone
by Trump
and his hard right minions
the end of diversity
means the end of pluralism
the end of equality
the end of concern for everybody
we all need to speak up
loud and clear
scream and shout
we are all done if we don't
end of my complaint

The Human Voice

the human voice is a superb instrument
surpasses all mechanical instruments
strings woodwinds percussions
non-duplicate the range of sound
the depth of feeling
the experience of listening
to the human voice
in a sense, the human voice is a miracle
how it was made
is beyond understanding
the only explanation for me
is something beyond explanation
divine transcendent
almost supernatural
we are as individuals
very fortunate that we are given the opportunity
to listen to what the human voice can convey
and a few very lucky people
are blessed with the gift of a singing voice

Arnold David Richards

Authorship

entering the world of authorship is an interesting experience
I don't write novels
I don't write plays
but I do try to write poetry
as best i can
of interest to some
but not everyone
writing is a challenge
the challenge of saying something
and saying it well
I often don't feel up to the challenge
but I keep trying
for some reason authorship
is one of the highest skills
but it takes a lot of work and a lot of practice
a lot of dedication
inspiration
information
the ability to place words
and sentences on a page
that will be edifying to others
and not fall flat
of course we have role models
substantial ones
Shakespeare was the ultimate playwright
Virgil was a very important poet
and Sappho

and then there's the whole list of modern poets
T.S. Eliot
W.H. Auden
e e cummings
Emily Dickinson
D.H. Lawrence
Sylvia Plath
Alan Ginsberg
the list is long
all of us aspire
for some recognition for our effort
and for our craft
we keep trying and sometimes succeed
in a very limited way
publishing what one has written
is very satisfying
it is a very good feeling
to hold a book in your hand
that you've published
and share it with others as well
I am grateful for any talent I have
and I am grateful for any recognition that I receive
writing poems or novels or plays
is a high form of communication
which we all should and do celebrate

Much Ado about Something

the world must be peopled
much ado about something
our progeny is our posterity
the ratio of births to deaths
needs to be a positive number
for us to survive
we have a major caring enterprise
we all participate
one way or the other
each doing our part
some directly
many indirectly
all creatures share
a biological imperative
to reproduce
parents take care of children
children grow up and take care of parents
and the world goes on

Last night on PBS they had a special devoted to Peter, Paul, and Mary, and one of the songs they presented was Deportee. Deportee was Woody Guthrie's last song and it was popularized by Pete Seeger and Joni Mitchell. It is clearly even more relevant now, with Trump's policies, than it was then when it was written after the crash of the airplane.

It made me think of my own history and connection with folk music.

It began my first year at the University of Chicago. There was a folk music group of students, Stone, Stein, and Gottesman who sang on the train called the *Pacemaker* on the trip from Chicago to New York at Christmas time. I remember a concert by Sonny Terry and Brownie McGhee. Sonny Terry plays the harmonica and Brownie McGhee the guitar. Folk music was very much part of the University of Chicago community. We listened to Woody Guthrie and Pete Seeger, Lead Belly and Blind Lemon Jefferson. I remember when we returned to New York we went to Leadbelly's last sessions at his home. I think it was in the Bronx. My interests ranged widely. We had a good friend who was a friend of Eric Weissman, the banjo player from the Journeymen, who we knew personally as well. We listened to Richard Dyer Bennett, as well as the more classic folk music. We also liked bluegrass and went to concerts in Virginia when we lived in Petersburg. Folk music was very much part of our connection to our children. I remember singing with them the song Abiyoyo, a song with an African melody and lyrics by Pete Seeger.

Our interest in Bob Dylan, the Rolling Stones, the Beatles evolved from our folk music interest. There were women singers that we followed: Jean Ritchie and her dulcimer, Joni Mitchell, Joan Baez, Carly Simon, and others. Folk music was very much part of the Vietnam demonstrations. Folk music, with the songs of protest, and folk music in general is emotional and makes life meaningful unlike any other music.

Man and Woman

the connection between
a man and a woman
may be automatic
or maybe problematic
love at first sight happens
but not that often
a deep relationship
takes a lot of work
a lifetime commitment
should not be entered into casually
and once a connection is made
it takes a lot of work to maintain
when achieved,
it is a gift to be treasured
we have been married seventy-one years
lucky us

Arnold David Richards

Aspire

I aim higher
satisfying desire
pleasing others
gratifying wishes
making a difference
fulfilling dreams
recognition
appreciation
self-fulfillment
creative
accomplishments
all that I ask for
to go one more time
into the fray

Trump

everyone should recognize
that Trump is profoundly un-American
a threat to our democracy
a threat to the rule of law
a threat to the constitution
a threat to our judiciary
a threat to our academic institutions
a threat to our individual freedom
a would-be dictator
will we stand up?
now or never
an end to my anti-MAGA song

Democracy

free speech
and free thought
are foundational for democracy
both are at risk right now
we have a would be dictator
as president
and a complacent electorate
the combination is very scary
and the remedy is not evident
we need a national dialogue
a national conversation
on this subject
it should happen in the Congress
but it won't
it should happen in the press
but that seems unlikely as well
the people need to be involved
on the grassroots level
town hall meetings everywhere
a committee should be organized
to begin the process of finding venues
we are awfully uneducated
in regard to democratic values
this has to change
sooner rather than later

Suffering

Aristotle said knowledge comes from suffering
I would say poetry comes from suffering
poetry requires engagement
and engagement always includes some pain
the alternative is complacency
inaction noninvolvement
insulation isolation
not possible unless one shuts out all the media
stop reading newspapers
and disconnect from all the news of the world
in which bad things happen
to good people
and bad people
poetry helps making
the meaningless
meaningful
so we can go on living

Arnold David Richards

Love

love is what makes the world go round?
banal but profound
reciprocity is the key
do to the other, as the other would do to me
too often honored in the breach
the promise not the doing
connecting each to each
makes everyone stronger
may even make everyone live longer
caring and commitment
for a moment or a lifetime
gratifying
and edifying
follow your heart

Intimacy

is hard to achieve
requires a degree of honesty
and obliteration of our
personal identity
that is hard to come by
naturally
but is necessary
for a derp relationship
which all of us yearn for
and some of us are lucky to achieve

Arnold David Richards

Affirmation

Musk
the man who would be king
new political party
end of Trump
end of MAGA
good for the country
good for us
affirmation

Civilization

is very fragile
we are close
to the tipping point
annihilation
or survival
nuclear Armageddon
is closer than we think
reason and good will
may not suffice
tyrants
dictators
have their own agendas
theirs not ours
end of my sad song ends

Arnold David Richards

Song

I sing a song of love
heart and soul
I sing of heart
I sing of soul
all encompassing
my reach is wide
I touch many
who are touched by me
gratified
edified
treasured
loved

Beauty

the appreciation of beauty
is a profoundly human ability
which we do not share with other creatures
it makes our existence transcendent
we have a consciousness outside of ourselves
it is not something we are born with
it has to be developed
learned nurtured
by experience
achievable
in time
meaning and beauty
are our reason for existing
and the ultimate
gratification

Arnold David Richards

Song 2

I will sing you a song
it is not very long
it is about our country
that we all love
and need to protect
from dictators
and demagogues
who would take our
freedom
and our liberty
end the rule of law
end the independence
of our academic institutions
our courts
our cultural institutions
our free press
where is Edward R. Murrow?
we need him desperately

Our World

we have to acknowledge
there are people in the world
that are self-serving
and selfish
they want others to do for them
and not that they to do for others
more concerned about their financial bottom line
then their moral bottom line
they don't believe in altruism
they can be hating and hateful
and hurtful
a better world without these people,
but we have to learn to live with them

Arnold David Richards

Respect

relationships require
mutual respect
but respect has to be deserved
respect has to be earned
it cannot be based on convenience
it has to be based on commitment
and on the concern for the best interests of all
bad things happen to good people
and good people need the support of their friends
and friends respect people who support them
and come to their side when they are attacked
even if it is difficult
it is hard to respect people
who take the easy way out
and don't stand up for what is right

Empathy

empathy
is what makes us human
feeling for the other person
connects us
in a very special way
widens our world
broadens our perspective
we are better for it
imagine a world
in which the capacity for empathy
is shared by most
we are nicer to each other
less anger
less hate
less pain

Creativity

promoting creativity
is a great achievement
a very high human good
great for the creator
great for the enabler
great for all
who are touched
by new sensibilities
new feelings
new insights
new understandings
moves the world forward
for the benefit of all

Sadism and Masochism

are twin evils
pleasure from hurting others
and pleasure from hurting oneself
driven by anger and guilt
distorted human relationships
both are driven by a need to be in charge
and in control
often a response to serious trauma
and disappointment
punishment of
the other
and the self
self-understanding is the answer
love is the answer

Arnold David Richards

Nostalgia

poignant memories
how many madeleines
will it take to recover the past
six friends in high school
Erasmus Hall
three went to Harvard
two to the U of C
one to Radcliffe
five still alive
one gone
loved
remembered
missed
nostalgia
won't bring him back

Life and Love

what is the difference between loving
and liking ?
loving is emotional
liking is rational
loving is inspirational
liking is reasonable
loving is permanent
liking is ephemeral
what is best is when they are together
loving someone you like
liking someone you love
then you have it all

Arnold David Richards

Dreams

dreams are a wonder
and a mystery
the filing cabinet of our mind
decides what to remember and what to forget
who was the author?
our creative unconscious
more poetic than our waking state
wishes are the driver
love and hate
libido and aggression
the cast of characters
are from our childhood
parents siblings
intense
and casual ones
the narratives are original
like a novel
or a play

Dream 2

dreams are a wonder
and a mystery
the filing cabinet of our mind
decides what to remember and what to forget
who was the author?
our creative unconscious
more poetic than our waking state
wishes are the driver
love and hate
libido and aggression
the cast of characters
are from our childhood
parents siblings
intense relationship relationships
and casual ones
the narratives are original
like a novel
or a play
what is essential is the visual
pictures not words
what we see not what we hear
we spend the night
looking at our dreams
watching a movie in our sleep

Arnold David Richards

often anxious
very scary sometimes
then we wake up
it's only a dream

The Body

the body is a mystery
a wonder
and a miracle
many moving parts
all work together
in synchrony
and harmony
the maker outdid Himself
with this creation
it comes in many varieties,
male and female
and many colors
vanilla and chocolate
but the greatest achievement
is the capacity for self-awareness
we are up and doing
able to influence the world
change the world
change your environment
plan for the future
remember the past
AI can try to imitate us
but it has its work cut out for it
and ultimately cannot succeed
in my opinion

Arnold David Richards

My Father

I go to sleep
I see my father
I hear his voice
I feel his presence
it is an experience
that can be had by only one generation
two at most
needs to be preserved
in words

Father's Day

Father's Day
is my day
one day
but it should be every day
not just one day
I see my father
role as special because my children are special
enduring growing
becoming more meaningful as time goes on
we grow together and separately
we become more alike and more different
treasured and cherished
our shared humanity
sustain us

Arnold David Richards

Sic Transit Gloria

sic transit gloria
we all have one day in the sun
when we are noticed and applauded
for what we've said and done
but it is ephemeral passes quickly
and we are replaced by the next player
who enters from the dark
and makes his or her mark
noticed in the next day
we all take turns
when we have it
and not regret when it's lost

Poetry

I have a gift
I can express profound thoughts
and deep emotions
with a few words
it is a recent development
it does not have a long history
where it comes from is a mystery
some connection to self analysis
requires self-awareness
and connection with my surround
words are meaningful
and felicitous
I write for myself
for others and for my posterity
I am establishing a record
which I can share with others
it is the most satisfying activity that I can think of
it drives me. it sustains me.
I sleep peacefully
and I feel engaged every minute of the day
my poetic mind beats like my corporeal heart

Arnold David Richards

Socrates

I identify with Socrates
who was asked to drink hemlock
his crime corrupting the youth of Athens
I was asked to resign from NYPSI
my crime
corrupting the members by
my progressive anti-establishment views
I am corrupting the younger members
who need to march lockstep with those
in charge
Socrates discussed the immortality of the soul
before he drank the poison
I talk about the immortality of my ideas
after I resigned

NYPSI needs me
more than I need them
I will win in the end
the future belongs
to those on my side
NYPSI may not survive

Plato

Platon in Greek
means broad
broad shoulders
broad thought
after Socrates died
he started an academy
Does NYPSI need a new institute
After I was expelled
Plato wrote dialogues
I write poems
NYPSI is impoverished
by my loss
does anyone care
another day
another poem

Arnold David Richards

Disorder

disorder is disturbing
for most
order is calming for all
uncertainty is upsetting
certainty is soothing
we don't like surprises
it was calm in the beginning
floating in the womb
and then being taken care of
after we get born
but we need to learn to take care of ourselves
disturbances in the world abound
we need to be always vigilant
but our capacity for self-protection is limited
we do best
with a lot of help from others
safety in unity
but some dangers may be overwhelming
we are small players
in a very dangerous world

Poems

I write poems to connect
with people
connection requires empathy
empathy is essential
you need to have some sense
about what is going on
in the other person's mind
what are they thinking
what are they feeling
it is helped
by our common humanity
are common experiences
our common needs
and desires
all those mesh
and connection becomes meaningful
emotional not theoretical
real not hypothetical
lasting and enduring
our sense of humanity
is here to stay

Arnold David Richards

The Golden Mean

450 BC was the height of Greek civilization
democracy
the golden mean
restraint
the *Venus de Milo*

What Keeps a Man Alive

what keeps a man alive
care and concern for others
introspection
self-observation
connection
selflessness
principles
ideals
commitment
to fairness
justice
equality
inclusion
all of the above
in any order
makes a good life
and hopefully
a long life
we live
and are well

Arnold David Richards

Life Poem

my mind soars
as my body sinks
my thoughts are infinite
my time is limited
my mind is strong.
my flesh is weak.
there is no escape
from nature's constraints
the truth hurts
I am the way I was made
and I will be that way
until my grave

Aspire

aspire
aim higher
aim for success
success is better
than failure
winning is better than
losing
form alliances
make connections
live a good life
for all to see

Arnold David Richards

Destiny

anatomy is destiny
geography is necessity
but what counts most
is personality
how we relate to others
and how we relate to ourselves
self-esteem
is the bottom line
the rest is commentary
self-esteem
separates the winners
from the losers
those who succeed
and those who fail

Tyranny

tyranny
at home is what
Trump is after
sending marines
to L.A. is first salvo
more will follow
where is the opposition
loyal or disloyal
our body politic
is numb
passive
helpless
courts may try
and meet with defiance
from Trump
are we aware
that our democracy
our liberty
and our way of life
is at stake

Arnold David Richards

I Prefer Fame to Fortune

fame can last
there are no pockets in the shroud
fame can grow
the bottom line
waxes and wanes
fame is meaningful
money is the ephemeral
fame is substantive
fortune comes and goes
fame is honest
fortune may be ill acquired
the choice for me is clear
fame over fortune
now and forever

What Was Was

what is is
what will be will be
denial and memory
are the twin antipodes
for dealing with trauma
losses and gains
pleasure and pain
denial distorts
the narrative
unless overcome
so we can know what is true
the old and the new
what was was
what is is
is here to stay

Arnold David Richards

Mistakes

it is essential
that we learn
from our mistakes
better if we don't make
them in the first place
but mistakes are inevitable
for all of us
but if we succeed
in looking at them objectively
we can be ahead of the game
mistakes should not be buried
as they often are
mistakes should not be ignored
which may be easy to do

be honest
be true
best for you

Topsy Turvey

life is like
a teeter-totter
up and down
high and low
all around
a surround
we need to find our place
where is best
where to stand
where to lay
where to walk
where to run
where to cry
where to shout
where to sing
where to ring
the brown bells of
Merthyr

Arnold David Richards

Extinction

are we at the edge of extinction
nuclear clock
close to midnight
ticking since 1945
Iran has the will
do they have the way
who will have the last word
whose rational self-interest
will prevail
ours is clear
is theirs?

Harmony

we sing on the same note
we are together
unison
harmony
easily
connected
two are one
life goes on
almost
forever

Arnold David Richards

Holocaust

from the gas chambers
to the crematorium
is a short distance
Germans killed 6 million Jews
of a large cohort of German Nazis
only a few were punished
most returned to high places
some went to the United States
and built rockets
no guilt, no remorse
outrageous
a shame on all of us

Lucky Me

I am a very lucky guy
I shouldn't boast
I should worry about the evil eye
but I don't believe in magic
I am thankful for all I have been given
for all the love
all the admiration
all the approval
and for all the love I have received
I am grateful that
I have been able to give to others
I am grateful for all my achievements
that matter
for now
and more to come
lucky me

Arnold David Richards

1933

Hitler becomes Chancellor
25,000 books are burned mostly by Jewish authors
40,000 watch the book burning
the beginning of Nazi propaganda
the end of Western civilization
which does not return until 1945

Poetry 2

two poems a day are
better than one
poems are what drives me
poetry sustains me
writing poetry is like praying
connecting with the divine
reaching for the sublime
and the ordinary
quotidian

Choice

choice is what defines us
choice is essential for democracy
especially for women
reproductive rights are basic
each one of us needs to assure
that we can choose what we need
and decide what to do
in all aspects of our life
the end of democracy
the beginning of dictatorship
begins with the loss of choice

Poem

brevity is the soul of wit
less is more
precision
is better than
obfuscation
economy
communication
is a challenge
for all

Arnold David Richards

Perpetrators

at the end of WW II
many perpetrators
were not punished
they were given
high places in Germany
a few were found guilty
but not enough

Nazis to save us
from the Russians
unconscionable

Presidency

imperial presidency
ineffective legislature
reckless judiciary
our democracy is in danger
our constitution is in danger
our country is in danger
who will speak up?
who will act?
who will save us?
can we save ourselves?

Arnold David Richards

Global Warming

global warming
is a warning
for our planet
climate change
will lead to
our extinction
we need to act now

or it will be too late
for our future
the ball is in our court
act now
or never
our choice
while our
habitat
is still in place
but not forever

If You Will It

if you will it
even a broom
can shoot
Yiddish optimism
defies reality
comes from necessity
in a dangerous world
hope sustains us
staying alive
is the ultimate triumph
against the odds

Arnold David Richards

Extinction

it is very hot
we are at the brink
of extinction
corals gone
sea rising
cities under water
we can't get
our act together
fossil fuels
now and forever
there are solutions
if we care
blow the bugles
bang the drum
action by
everyone

1984

1984
came and went
not over yet
Orwell had no idea
how bad it could get
freedom fragile
choices shrinking
what can one think
about the future
big brother
here to stay
too many
like it that way

Arnold David Richards

Paris

Pa Ris

for fun
for sport
a joke
the name of a city
Paris
where everyone
tries to have fun
one on one
and together
cancan
dance all night
from dusk
to dawn
life is short
make the most of it
when you can
before it is
over

Questions

why is there something
and not nothing ?
what is the beginning
and what is the end ?
these are the cosmological questions
that we can't answer
but we can't be at peace
until we do
our knowledge is limited
is there a higher power
that has answers
we hope there is
that is what religion is about

Don't Ask for the Moon

don't ask for the moon
when you have the stars
aim higher
aspire
you can have more
you can have it all
if you want all
the limit
is in your mind

Past

the past is present in memory
memory provides continuity
continuity is legacy
we preserve the past
for the next generation
to learn from
to celebrate
to appreciate
all our accomplishments
the good we have done
and the help we have given
to many others
each one of us
makes a contribution
to our mutual humanity
ever more

Arnold David Richards

Ars longa vita brevis

art is long
and life is short
it takes a long time
to acquire a skill
patience
persistence
and determination
it determines
the human condition
which we all must
abide by

on the other hand
works of art
may last a long time
achieve permanence
a Mozart symphony
a Shakespeare sonnet
will be with us
as long as we can hear
and as long as we can see
an abiding source of pleasure
and satisfaction
for many
if not all

Big Battalions

victory
belongs to the big battalions
said Sigmund Freud
but who made him an expert?
I think he was very much aware
that life is not fair
but sometimes underdogs do succeed
when they have the better arguments
and logic and reason on their side
not just numbers
there was David who killed Goliath
brain over brawn
a lesson for us all

Arnold David Richards

Mythology

all of us
have our mythologies
who we are
where we came from
we make our parents
more important
than they are
we aggrandize
the history
of our country
we exaggerate our
achievements
we make ourselves
more important
for other people
than we are for them
but in the back of our minds
we know the truth
all of us are
very ordinary

Risk

life is risk
and risk taking
is part of life
avoiding risk taking
leads to stagnation
nothing ventured
nothing gained
is banal
but profoundly true

Maidel and Me

Maidel and me
Arlene makes three
we are a family
shared activities
shared sensibilities
shared emotions
love and devotion
love for now and
evermore

Reality

reality
is what we live by
it provides constraints
offers no forgiveness
the past cannot be recovered
the future cannot be assured
beggars cannot ride
we can wish for anything
and be disappointed
again and again
reality cannot be ignored
wishes are not horses
and we cannot ride

Ambition

ambition drives
all of us
we strive to succeed
we strive to acquire things
we strive for fame
and fortune
until we learn
both are ephemeral
and not always
meaningful
what counts
is the here and now
of relationships
which are lasting
and grow with time
with young and old
we can transmit
our values
and that is the most satisfying
defines who we are
and who we want to be
agency
its what makes
the world go round
agency is how
we find our place
save one life
save the world

Grief

grief is healing
grief is revealing
once you know the source of your pain
your life is not the same
you can undo
what needs to be undone
you can make amends
set the record straight
compensate
whoever deserves compensation
one small sorry
can go a long way

1934

The Fuhrer and me
born in the same year
1934
I entered the world
he became chancellor
I think that stamped my life
history is my passion
World War II and the Holocaust
are always with me
on my mind by day
my concentration camp nightmares at night
my determination to oppose demagogues
wherever they arise
defending our Constitution and the role of law
which is under attack now
by Trump and his supporters
fighting the good fight
with all my heart and might

Poem

the power of the pen
the pen can protect us
Tom Paine wrote
Common Sense
spoke truth to power
opposed autocracy
an argument for democracy
and equality
for nothing to fear
but fear itself
our Declaration of Independence
our challenge to King George
in 1776 Uncle Sam was born
250 years ago
and here we are now
our home-grown man
who would be king

Arnold David Richards

Music

music
pours in your ear
from a voice
or an instrument
permeates
your body
and your soul
every corner
of your being
hearing is a miracle
music is inspired
makes life worth living
return in singing
for all to hear

Lieutenant Kijé

when something is heard today
when it was first heard is remembered
memory connects the present with the past
memory provides continuity to life
Lieutenant Kijé suite played on WQXR
was written in 1934
the year I was born
I must have heard it again
when I was ten
On WQXR
Or WNYC
life is a tapestry
of memories
interwoven
like a patchwork quilt
the patches are connected
sewn together
many suites
Lieutenant Kijé is one of many
still stirring now
as it was when first heard
filed in my musical playbook
my sensibilities change
as I grow older
but my appreciation
remains

Arnold David Richards

Psyche

for Strachey it was psyche
for Freud it was soul
libido is passion
ego is I
instinct is drive
Freud understands human motivation
the language of feeling
not scientism
humanism
Freud's gift

Two Gods that Failed

my father was a Bolshevik
his God communism
was killed by Stalin
and his purge trials
he became a Zionist
Israel was founded
my God Zionism
was killed by Bibi
the war criminal
two Gods that failed

Arnold David Richards

Virtue

virtue is its own reward
satisfaction comes from knowing
you did the right thing
there is gratification in
pleasing others
true in the best of all possible worlds
true for Candide
but often honored in the breach
in my experience
no noble deed goes unpunished
a sad fact of life

AI

AI
will replace people
AI will build machines
people will write unredeeming poetry
wait on tables
be servants
entertainment
not production
AI will write papers
end of academia
gloomy prospect
end of my song

Arnold David Richards

Bastille Day

Bastille day
July 14
celebrates the French Revolution
The end of the monarchy
we need a Bastille day
in the USA
to celebrate the end of the man
who would be king
and take away our liberty
and end equality
and does not believe in the rule of law
does not believe in checks and balances
rise up
let's hear the people sing

Trump

Trump crazy
the Canadian Prime Minister says
a world order without us
we become a fourth world country
no clout
no influence
a failing economy
a bankrupt foreign policy
end of the American century
one person can destroy it all
but I blame most those who voted for him
put him into power
he will be with us as long as he is alive and
then Vance and worse will follow

Arnold David Richards

Poem 4

Arlene and me
Maidel makes three
we are family
we hang out and play
happiness is a warm puppy
together

Our Planet

in the beginning
our planet was pristine
only natural vegetation
then came people
the constructor
the pyramids
the Hanging Gardens of Babylon
the Library at Alexandria
the Colossus at Rhodes
then more recent structures
skyscrapers
bridges
and boxes
made of tacky-tacky
all look just the same
we are what we build
architecture defines us
Renaissance Alberti
21st century Frank Gehry
today
what will we build tomorrow?

Arnold David Richards

Commentary

poems are
comments on life
approval
and disapproval
major and minor
good and bad
and indifferent
details
attention must be paid
the salesman's wife said
before he died

Empathy

Dostoyevsky said
if you feel the pain of others
you are human
profound wisdom
something we all need to live by
provides a road map for our relationships
inability of others to do that as well
may derail our interactions
expect the best of people
but accept when they fall short
and avoid self-pity
at all costs

Writing Poems

writing poetry keeps me alive
intellectual stimulation,
emotional stimulation
prevents stagnation
my heart beats faster
my mind churns
thoughts fly
poems are ideas
ideas grow
poems grow
writing poetry
can become a matter of
life or death
an awesome gift

Trump and Bolsonaro

Bolsonaro wanted to
set up a theocratic fascist state in Brazil
Trump's state is fascist
not yet theocratic
but they have a lot in common
Bolsonaro tried to have his successor assassinated
he is in jail
Trump is trying to get him released
how low
Can Trump go?

Arnold David Richards

Me

I am a very unusual person
I don't know anyone like me
my wife doesn't know anybody
like me also
I don't know why she puts up with me
she says it is because she loves me
I am a challenge
I never stop
24/7 and sleep
exhausting
I only stop to breathe

www.ingramcontent.com/pod-product-compliance
Lightning Source LLC
Chambersburg PA
CBHW061704120626
46550CB00003B/1078